Liliuokalani

The Last Queen of Hawaii

Liliuokalani
The Last Queen of Hawaii

by John MacGregor

Illustrated by Pamela Johnson

Scholastic Inc.
New York Toronto London Auckland Sydney
Mexico City New Delhi Hong Kong Buenos Aires

*To Ken Bishé, David Hessler, Dr. Louise Maxwell,
Dr. Denise Brown-Allen, and Gillian Branigan, who taught me
to appreciate the importance of history. And to Ralph Pacifico,
who taught me to appreciate the importance of hard work.*
—J. M.

*For Imani, Jeffrey, Lema, Polynesia,
Joseph, and Isabella Giovanna*
—P. J.

ISBN-13: 978-0-545-07081-2
ISBN-10: 0-545-07081-3

12 11 10 9 8 7 6 5 4 3 2 1   9 10 11 12 13 14/0

Printed in the U.S.A.
First printing, March 2009
Book design by Jennifer Rinaldi Windau

Contents

Introduction

Aloha! What do you know about Hawaii? You may know that it is made up of islands. You may have heard about Hawaii's hula dancers, palm trees, pineapples, and beautiful beaches.

You may have learned that Captain Cook landed his ships on those islands in 1778. You might know that Hawaii

Japan

United
States

Hawaii

Australia

Kauai

Oahu

Molokai

Maui

Lanai

Hawaii

became the fiftieth state of the United States on August 21, 1959.

But Hawaii was not always part of the United States. The native Hawaiian people have a long and rich history of their own. They have their own music, customs, and traditions. They have a beautiful native language.

At one time, Hawaii was an independent country with its own royal government. But starting in the nineteeth century, a group of Americans wanted to take over the kingdom of Hawaii. They wanted Hawaii for its sugar crop. They wanted to fight Hawaii's proud and strong queen, Queen Liliuokalani (lih-lee-ooh-woh-kah-**lah**-nee).

The Americans won the fight, and Queen Liliuokalani had to step down from the Hawaiian throne. She was the last queen of Hawaii. This is her story.

Chapter One

A Queen Is Born

On September 2, 1838, a baby girl was born near Punchbowl Hill in Honolulu, Hawaii. Her mother's name was Keohokalole and her father's name was Kapaakea. They both came from families of Hawaiian royal chiefs.

Punchbowl Hill

Her father was the chief of the village. They lived in a large, grass house that was surrounded by smaller huts. The baby was born into a large family. She had nine brothers and sisters.

The baby girl was named Liliu Loloku Walania Kamakaeha. That is quite a big name for a little girl! When she grew up, she would become known as Queen Liliuokalani. But for now, she was called Liliu. When Liliu was two, her family began calling her Lydia Paki.

Here's how little Lydia got her very long name:

According to Hawaiian custom, the honor of naming the new baby was given to the highest-ranking female chief. The honor was given to a woman named Kinau. Hawaiian custom also said that Kinau could name the baby after something important that was going on in her life. Kinau had an eye infection at the time. She thought her infection was important enough for people to remember. So she named the baby girl Liliu Loloku Walania Kamakaeha after her eye infection!

Liliu means: smarting
Loloku means: tearful
Walania means: a burning pain
Kamakaeha means: the sore eye

13

When this baby girl was born, royal children were not raised by their own parents. They were sent to live with other parents who would take good care of them. The baby girl was wrapped in a soft blanket made out of bark and taken to her new parents. The baby girl's new parents were Paki and his wife, Konia. They loved her very much.

This Hawaiian custom of adoption was called **hanai**. Queen Liliuokalani said it was hard to explain hanai to people who weren't native Hawaiians. But for Hawaiians, hanai was a beautiful custom. It spread friendship, love, and community among the chiefs and their people. The parents all loved their adopted children as if they were their own.

Lydia Paki went to the Chiefs' Children's School, which was also called the Royal School, when she was

Royal School

four years old. The Royal School was run by two American missionaries, Amos Cooke and his wife, Juliette. The school was near Iolani Palace. King Kamehameha III had given the land to the Cookes for the school.

Lydia was carried to school on her first day by her babysitter, a nice woman named Kaikai. She rode to school on Kaikai's shoulders. Lydia was scared at first. She was worried about being away from Paki and Konia. But when the other children came out to meet her, she wasn't afraid anymore.

Three of Lydia's classmates at the Royal School would later become kings of Hawaii:

Alexander Liholiho became King Kamehameha IV.
Lot Kamehameha became King Kamehameha V.
William Charles Lunalilo became King Lunalilo.

All of the children at the Royal School were related to the kings and queens of Hawaii. Many of them became famous people in Hawaiian history.

Lydia was one of the youngest students. She learned English at the Royal School. Now Lydia spoke her native Hawaiian language—and English, too!

Hawaiian is a beautiful language. Here are some Hawaiian words and their definitions:

'aina (**eye**-nuh) land, earth

aloha (ah-**low**-ha) hello, good-bye, love, affection

hula (**hoo**-la) a Hawaiian dance

kai (kai) sea, seawater

kama 'aina (**ka**-ma **eye**-nuh) native-born

kanaka maoli (ka-**nah**-kuh **mao**-lee) full-blooded Hawaiian perso

lei (lay) chain, wreath of flowers

mahalo (ma-**ha**-low) thanks, gratitude

mele (**may**-lay) song, anthem, poem

'ohana (oh-**ha**-nuh) family, relative

'ukulele (you-koo-**lay**-lay) a small guitar

wai (why) water or liquid that's not seawater

wikiwiki (**wee**-key-**wee**-key) fast, hurry

Lydia lived at the Royal School. She didn't go home at night. She went to class every day and went to church every Sunday. The children marched to church in two lines, boys and girls side by side. The oldest children went first, so Lydia was always at the end of the line.

Lydia missed Paki and Konia. And she thought the food at the Royal School was terrible! She was used to delicious Hawaiian food, and she did not think the Cookes gave the children enough to eat. For supper, she had bread with molasses. Sometimes the children would sneak into the garden at night and look for roots or vegetables. That's how hungry they were! Lydia was very happy when she could go to her friend's house and eat delicious Hawaiian food, such as *kulolo*, *paipaiee*, and *koele-palau*.

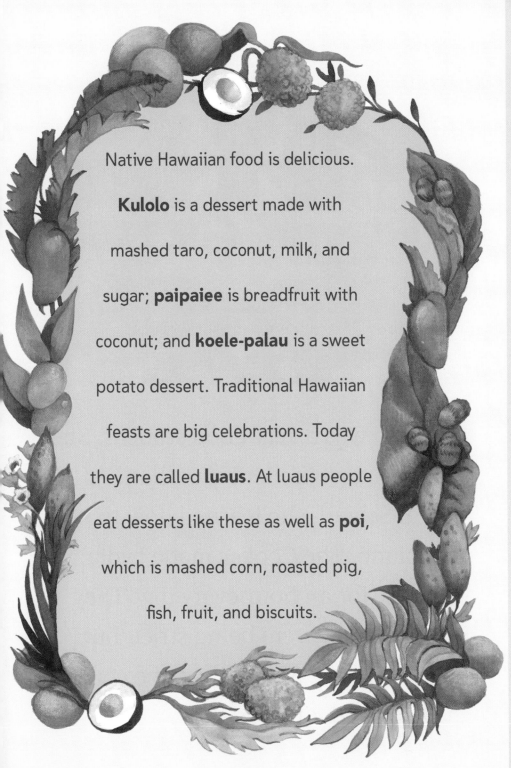

Native Hawaiian food is delicious.

Kulolo is a dessert made with mashed taro, coconut, milk, and sugar; **paipaiee** is breadfruit with coconut; and **koele-palau** is a sweet potato dessert. Traditional Hawaiian feasts are big celebrations. Today they are called **luaus**. At luaus people eat desserts like these as well as **poi**, which is mashed corn, roasted pig, fish, fruit, and biscuits.

Lydia was a very good student. She was also an excellent musician. At the Royal School, she learned how to play the piano. The Cookes made Lydia practice for an hour every day. They thought they were being strict, but Lydia loved it! She wished she could have played longer.

There was a fence around the Royal School. American boys used to peek over the fence to look at the royal children who would one day be the kings and queens of Hawaii. One of these boys was named John Owen Dominis. Years later, John became Lydia's husband!

Chapter Two
Liliuokalani Grows Up

When she was twelve years old, the Royal School closed and Lydia went to a new day school in Honolulu. Now she could go home at night to Paki and Konia. She was very happy.

Lydia noticed that many changes had taken place in Honolulu. It didn't look like the same place she had left when she was four years old. There were no more grass huts! Now there were big, fancy buildings. Native

Hawaiians had sold a lot of their land to white Americans from New England. Life was changing in Hawaii.

In 1848, King Kamehameha III was advised by foreigners to divide up the land: one part for the kings, one part for the government, and one part for the common people. This was called the Great Mahele, a division of lands. It took the land from the kings and allowed foreigners to buy it from the common people and to control it through the government. It was a big change for native Hawaiians.

But Lydia still loved her traditional Hawaii. She visited all the islands. She went to Kealakekua Bay, where there is a memorial statue to Captain James Cook.

In 1778, Captain Cook landed with his two ships, *Discovery* and *Resolution*. The native Hawaiians thought he was one of their gods, Lono. At first they welcomed him. They honored Cook and his men with gifts and food. Eventually, the Hawaiians became suspicious and realized that Captain Cook could not be a god. In the end, they fought and Captain Cook was killed.

Captain James Cook

Hawaiians were polytheists, which means that they believed in more than one god. Here are some of the Hawaiian gods and what they represented:

Hina   goddess of the moon

Kanaloa   god of the sea

Kane   the creator

Ku   god of war

Lono   god of peace

Pele   goddess of the volcano

Ku

Lydia visited Mauna Loa, the world's largest volcano. She called it "one of the greatest natural wonders of the modern world." Visitors to Mauna Loa toss chains of flowers called *leis* into the flowing lava. The leis are gifts to Pele, the ancient goddess of fire.

Mauna Loa

Mauna Loa means "long mountain." It is the largest volcano on earth. In 1880, when Liliuokalani was visiting there, Mauna Loa erupted for eleven straight months.

Lydia continued to love music. When she was in school, her teachers let her lead the music class. Lydia also wrote many songs. When she was older, she composed a Hawaiian national anthem. Her most famous piece is a love song called "Aloha Oe."

The song "Aloha Oe" is about Lydia's love for Hawaii. Here are some of the words to the song:

Sweet memories come back to me
Bringing fresh remembrance of the past.
Dearest one, yes, you are mine own.
From you, true love shall never depart.

Here are some other songs written by Lydia:

Nani Na Pua Koolau	Beautiful Are the Flowers of Koolau
Ahe Lau Makani	The Soft, Gentle Breeze
Puna Paia Aala	Puna's Fragrant Bower
He Pule	A Prayer
Ka Wai Mapuna	The Water Springs
Kuu Pua I Paoakalani	My Flower at Paoakalani
He Inoa No Kaiulani	A Name Song for Kaiulani
Kokohi	To Hold Forever

Lydia's life was very busy and full. She traveled around Hawaii. She created a school for young people. In 1860, Lydia became engaged to an American man named John Owen Dominis. She married him two years later, at the age of twenty-four. Lydia and John had known each other for many years. He was one of the American boys who looked over the fence into the Royal School when they were children!

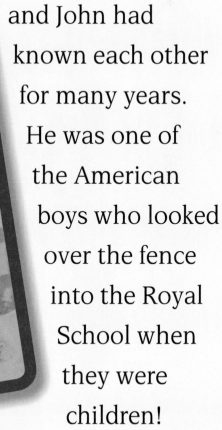

John Dominis

In April 1877, Lydia became the official heir to the Hawaiian throne. If anything happened to her brother, King Kalakaua, she would become the queen of Hawaii. Lydia was too small a name for such an important person. So she became known as Liliuokalani.

King Kalakaua

Here are the names of the kings and queen who ruled Hawaii:

King Kamehameha I   Ruled 1810–1819
(also known as Kamehameha the Great)

King Kamehameha II   Ruled 1819–1824
(also known as Liholiho)

King Kamehameha III   Ruled 1825–1854
(also known as Kauikeaouli)

King Kamehameha IV   Ruled 1855–1863
(also known as Alexander Liholiho)

King Kamehameha V   Ruled 1863–1872
(also known as Lot Kamehameha)

King Lunalilo   Ruled 1873–1874
(also known as William Charles Lunalilo)

King Kalakaua   Ruled 1874–1891
(also known as David La'amea Kalakaua)

Queen Liliuokalani   Ruled 1891–1893
(also known as Lydia Paki Liliuokalani)

Liliuokalani helped her brother King Kalakaua whenever he needed her. She tried to help him work with the American sugar planters and missionaries, who were called *haole* by the native Hawaiians. The haole were getting more powerful every day.

King Kalakaua sent Liliuokalani to England to represent Hawaii at the British queen's Golden Jubilee celebration. She had a wonderful time at the celebration. She met Queen Victoria and attended official parties at Buckingham Palace. But when she was in England, she got bad news! There was fighting in Hawaii. Liliuokalani immediately got on a boat to return to Honolulu.

Chapter Three
Becoming Queen

Liliuokalani returned home to find Hawaii in trouble. Her brother had lost his power. The Americans wanted to rule Hawaii. They wanted to control its sugar crop. King Kalakaua was forced to sign a new constitution.

View of Pearl Harbor

Iolani Palace

Soon after, King Kalakaua died. Liliuokalani believed that he died of a broken heart. He was so sad about what was happening to his country. Liliuokalani was named queen of Hawaii. Queen Liliuokalani moved into Iolani Palace.

Liliuokalani had every right to be the queen of Hawaii. She was a native Hawaiian. She was born to royal parents. She studied at the Royal School. Her brother had been the king. But the Americans did not want Hawaii to continue as a royal kingdom. They did not want Liliuokalani to be the queen. They did not want a queen at all. They wanted Americans to rule Hawaii.

From the moment Queen Liliuokalani took her throne, the Americans fought with her for control of Hawaii. They set up their own government.

They sent a battleship called the USS *Boston* to Honolulu. They sent soldiers and weapons to threaten the Hawaiian government.

USS Boston

Queen Liliuokalani knew that her little Hawaiian kingdom could not win a fight against the Americans. She did not want war on her island. So she surrendered. She stepped down as queen.

Liliuokalani was arrested by the Americans and held in prison in her own Iolani Palace. She was not allowed to have a royal title. She was no longer the queen. On July 4, 1894, the Republic of Hawaii was established. An American named Sanford Dole was named the president of the republic.

Liliuokalani and her companions made this quilt together while they were imprisoned in the palace. It is called a crazy quilt because it is made of many different colors and fabrics. In the center square of the quilt, they sewed these words: "Imprisoned at Iolani Palace . . . . We began the quilt here." It also includes the date: October 11, 1894.

Chapter Four
The Last Queen of Hawaii

Two years later, Liliuokalani was finally told that she was free. She took a boat to the United States and went to Washington, D.C. She tried to talk to President Grover Cleveland and members of the U.S. Congress about letting Hawaii be an independent country again. Liliuokalani stayed in the United States for two years.

During this time she wrote a book called *Hawaii's Story by Hawaii's Queen*. This book, published in 1898, soon became popular. In her book Liliuokalani explains the history of her country and how the American sugar planters and missionaries took over Hawaii.

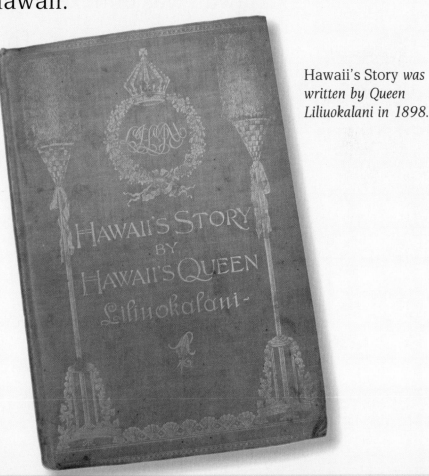

Hawaii's Story was written by Queen Liliuokalani in 1898.

Liliuokalani spent her whole life supporting Hawaii. She loved Hawaii. She did not believe it should have been taken over by Americans and become a part of the United States.

But Liliuokalani and her supporters did not win. On July 7, 1898, Hawaii was annexed to the United States. The Hawaiian flag flying over Iolani Palace was replaced by an American flag. There were fancy ceremonies to celebrate the annexation.

Liliuokalani was invited to the celebrations, but she refused to come. For Liliuokalani and other native Hawaiians, it was a sad, sad day.

Many people believe that the United States did not do the right thing for Hawaii. In 1993, one hundred years after Queen Liliuokalani's government was overthrown, the United States apologized to Hawaii. President Bill Clinton officially said the United States was sorry for the harm it had done to Hawaii.

On August 21, 1959, Hawaii became the fiftieth state.

This is part of what President Clinton signed into law:

"The Congress ... apologizes to Native Hawaiians on behalf of the people of the United States for the overthrow of the Kingdom of Hawaii on January 17, 1893 ... and the deprivation of the rights of Native Hawaiians to self-determination."

President Clinton signing the apology

Liliuokalani died in her house, Washington Place, on November 11, 1917, at the age of seventy-nine. She had no children of her own, but she left money to provide help to orphans and poor children in Hawaii. Her great work is carried out today through the Queen Liliuokalani Children's Center. She will always be remembered as a hero in Hawaii and its very last queen.

Liliuokalani statue at Iolani Palace

Glossary

annexation (an-eks-**a**-shuhn): when one country takes over another country

constitution (kon-stuh-**too**-shuhn): the system of laws in a country that state the rights of the people and the powers of the government

Great Mahele (grayt ma-**heh**-lay): a decision to redistribute land in Hawaii so that chiefs and commoners could own private land

hanai (huh-**nye**): a traditional Hawaiian custom in which a family adopts a chief's child and raises it as a family member

haole (**how**-lay): foreign or foreigner

koele palau (ko-eh-lay pa-**lau**): sweet potato pudding

kulolo (koo-**low**-low): Hawaiian dessert made from mashed taro and either grated coconut meat or coconut milk

lei (**lay**): a wreath of flowers that goes around the neck, like a necklace

missionary (**mish**-uh-ner-ee): someone who is sent by a church or religious group to teach that group's faith in a foreign country

paipaiee (pie-pie-**eh**-eh): a Hawaiian dessert that is made from coconut cream and breadfruit

poi (**poi**): a staple food in Hawaii, made by mashing cooked corn

republic (ri-**puhb**-lik): a country in which the head of the government is elected by the people